D1535231

/

Words of Love

Words of Love

Selected
by
Ben Whitley

HALLMARK EDITIONS

WORDS OF LOVE

The heart that loves
is always young.

GREEK PROVERB

The sea has its pearls,
The heaven its stars,
But my heart, my heart,
My heart has its love.

HEINRICH HEINE

Time is…
Too slow for those who wait,
Too swift for those who fear,
Too long for those who grieve,
Too short for those who rejoice;
But for those who love,
    time is not.

HENRY VAN DYKE

Love means the body, the soul,
the life, the entire being.

GUY DE MAUPASSANT

...while we live,
in love let's so persevere,
That when we live no more,
we may live ever.

ANNE BRADSTREET

Love is something eternal—
the aspect may change,
but not the essence.

VINCENT VAN GOGH

Love looks not with the eyes,
but with the mind.

WILLIAM SHAKESPEARE

Is it so small a thing
To have enjoyed the sun,
To have lived light in the spring,
To have loved,
To have thought,
To have done?

MATTHEW ARNOLD

I want not only to be loved,
but to be told that I am loved.

GEORGE ELIOT

In this my green world

Flowers birds are hands

They hold me

I am loved all day

All this pleases me

I am amused

I have to laugh from crying

Trees mountains are arms

I am loved all day

KENNETH PATCHEN

Love God, and do what you will.

SAINT AUGUSTINE

Love is the emblem of eternity:
it confounds all notion of time,
effaces all memory of a beginning,
all fear of an end.

MADAME DE STAËL

The water continually flowed and
flowed and yet it was always
there; it was always the same
and yet every moment it was new.

HERMANN HESSE

Beauty is not in the face;
Beauty is a light in the heart.

KAHLIL GIBRAN

...For I do love you...

as the dew loves the flowers;

as the birds love the sunshine;

as the wavelets love the breeze....

MARK TWAIN

If you wish to be loved, love.

SENECA

Absence is the enemy of love.

ITALIAN PROVERB

'Tis what I love determines
how I love.

GEORGE ELIOT

There's nothing half so sweet
in life as love's young dream.

THOMAS MOORE

Love is the great Asker.

D. H. LAWRENCE

Spring bursts today,
For Love is risen and all
the earth's at play....

CHRISTINA ROSSETTI

Two souls with but a single thought,
Two hearts that beat as one.

VON MUNCH BELLINGHAUSEN

A crowd is not a company, and faces
are but a gallery of pictures,
and talk but a tinkling cymbal,
where there is no love.

FRANCIS BACON

It is difficult to define love.
But we may say that in the soul,
it is a ruling passion; in the mind,
it is a close sympathy and affinity;
in the body, a wholly secret
and delicate longing
to possess what we love....

DUC DE LA ROCHEFOUCAULD

Love is the gentle smile upon
the lips of beauty.

KAHLIL GIBRAN

Time flies,
Suns rise
And shadows fall.
Let time go by.
Love is forever over all.

FROM AN OLD SUN DIAL

A loving heart is the truest wisdom.

CHARLES DICKENS

My bounty is as boundless
as the sea, my love as deep;
the more I give to thee,
the more I have, for both are infinite.

WILLIAM SHAKESPEARE

Only that day dawns
to which we are awake.

HENRY DAVID THOREAU

Who are wise in love,
Love most, say least.

ALFRED, LORD TENNYSON

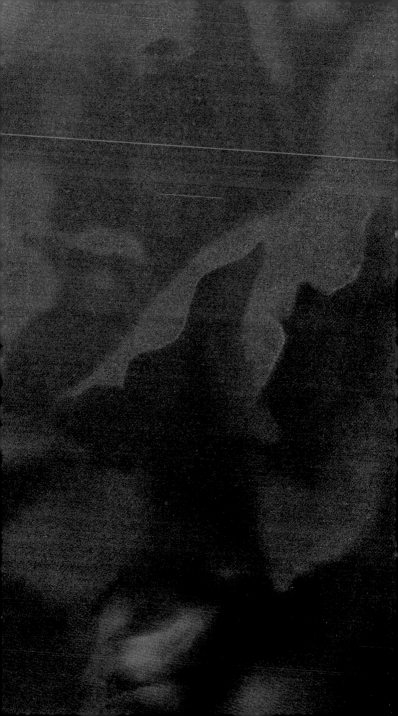

This is the true measure of love,
when we believe
that we alone can love,
that no one could ever
have loved so before us,
and that no one will ever love
in the same way after us.

JOHANN WOLFGANG VON GOETHE